MAKING
FANTASTIC JEWELRY

To Maurizio

Many thanks to:

Maurizio Minora, Filippo Minora, Marina Dell'Orto, Ezio Grazioli,
Donatella Zaccaria, Maria Pia Salfati, Lucio Loli

Giovanni Varenna, collector, for the yellow blender

my mother and sister

Editor: Cristina Sperandeo
Photography: Alberto Bertoldi
Translation: Chiara Tarsia
Graphic design and layout: Paola Masera and Amelia Verga with Beatrice Brancaccio

Library of Congress Cataloging-in-Publication Data Available

10 9 8 7 6 5 4 3 2 1

First paperback edition published in 2002 by
Sterling Publishing Co., Inc.
387 Park Avenue South, New York, NY 10016

Originally published in Italy under the title *Gioielli fai da te* by RCS Libiri S.p.A.
via Mecenate, 91, Milan, 20138

©1998 by RCS Libri S.p.A., Milano
I Edizione Grandi Manuali Fabbri ottobre 1998
English Translation © 2001 by Sterling Publishing
Distributed in Canada by Sterling Publishing
C/o Canadian Manda Group, One Atlantic Avenue, Suite 105
Toronto, Ontario, M6K 9E7, Canada
Distributed in Australia by Capricorn Link (Australia) Pty Ltd.
P.O. Box 704, Windsor, NSW 2756, Australia

Every effort has been made to ensure that all the information in this book is accurate. However, due to differir
conditions, and individual skills, the publisher cannot be responsible for any injuries, losses, and other dama
which may result from the use of the information in this book.

Sterling ISBN 0-8069-7941-0 Hardcover
         ISBN 1-4027-0124-1 Paperback

Paola Romanelli

MAKING
FANTASTIC JEWELRY

Sterling Publishing Co., Inc.
New York

CONTENTS

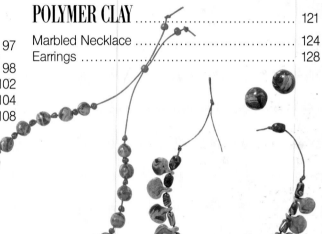

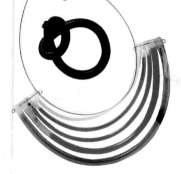

INTRODUCTION

The presence of jewels can be found throughout history. It is impossible, in fact, to indicate any civilization—whether sophisticated or primitive—in which jewels were not used for ornaments. Archeological findings give witness to the ancient, enduring presence of jewels in the past. A jewel is not merely a decorative element, but is also a means of communication. From a single jewel, we can learn the history of ancient man and the characteristics of contemporary human beings. Necklaces, bracelets, rings, and earrings aid us in identifying the tribe or race of origin, the official position, social class, civil status, etc. of their owners.

The materials that were used to make the jewelry tell us the level of craftsmanship reached by a particular society as well as their attributed value. The body, in all of its parts, finds in jewelry an ally that can be used to highlight or hide, defend or seduce—something, that is, that can share in the various cycles of existence.

AFRICA

In Africa everything is used for jewelry; all sorts of organic and mineral materials are worn on the body. On the one hand we find natural substances, such as ivory, bone, shell, amber, and coral, which are found in their natural state and are fairly simple to work with. On the other hand, there are also some materials that require more complex work processes. Wood, in the shades of brown, terracotta, and cream, is finely worked to make beads, or is cut into animal shapes. Wood is many times seen its original colorings, reminiscent of the desert, or brilliantly colored, recalling local fabrics. Bone has recently replaced ivory and is often accompanied by silver beads. The white spines of fishes are often used for simpler ornaments. The "cauri", a small shell, is often seen in African jewelry. Its scientific name is *Cypraea moneta*, and it appears to have originated in the Indian Ocean. It was first collected along the Maldives coast; it spread gradually towards Bengal and then arrived in Africa. These precious shells, already famous in the days of the Egyptian Pharos, were exchanged for gold, ivory, and slaves, and soon began to represent valuable currency. While the "cauri" were used as money, gold, instead, was used exclusively for jewelry ornaments. The most extraordinary examples are the earrings of the Mali women. These ornaments, four lobed and spiral shaped, can reach astonishing sizes and even weigh up to a pound. These earrings often lacerate their ear lobes; so, to avoid this from happening the women tie them to a cord of red thread and pass it over their heads, stretching it from ear to ear.

INDIA

India offers an extraordinary variety of jewels. From birth, the women are adorned with jewelry every moment of their lives. The people of India believe that jewels have the ability to make women into idols in addition to highlighting the grace of their movements. Bracelets, anklets, nose rings, and toe rings are a part of daily life and give a regal look, even to women of a modest standard of living who can only afford cheap materials such as glass or iron. Nature is often the source of inspiration for Indian jewelry. Numerous decorative motifs derived from flowers, seeds, and fruit are either interlaced or worked into metals. The splendid colors of glass, beads, and bracelets are inspired from the gaudy feathers of parrots, the blue tails of peacocks, and the yellow flowers of the mimosa. Silver is the most widely used metal throughout the entire Indian subcontinent, whether north or south, east or west. Beaten, engraved, or embossed, silver is often the only material used in making jewelry. It is also turned into beads of different shapes and sizes and alternated with other materials such as coral, turquoise, and amber. Silver is also used as a supporting element for setting semi-precious stones of various shapes and colors.

THE AMERICAS

Working precious metals was widespread in Latin America from the beginnings of the pre-Columbian civilizations. These peoples believed that gold was produced by the sun and silver from the tears of the moon. Expert goldsmiths have always used the techniques of hammering, melting, and chiseling to obtain real works of art. These precious metals were often worked to produce images of divinities—an example is the silver trinket bearing the likeness of the god Tumi, which is widely worn in Peru.

Terracotta is molded in Mexico into both geometrical and animal-shaped forms and is the basic material for certain kinds of jewelry.

South American Indians widely practice the goldsmith's art, which they learned from Spanish craftsmen. Here, silver is certainly the favored metal and it is often used as a background for turquoise overlays and mosaics. Natural materials such as tortoise carapace and black coral are still used to make bracelets, trinkets, and necklaces.

In the Amazon, bird feathers and beetle shells provide the means for making jewelry ornaments.

In Brazil even the children plait leather cords and produce complex and diversely colored decorations.

BEADS

Beads were made and used more than 40,000 years ago and are a characteristic of all cultures on all the continents.

At first natural materials, easily available, were used and worked by hand, such as bone, ivory, wood, stone chips, and shells. Later, glass became produced by industrial techniques that gave rise to the mass production of beads and to the creation of masterpieces with mosaics in miniature.

From one continent to another, particular models and production techniques have developed over the centuries.

The mass production of beads, especially by industries using low-cost materials, has created a huge selection for many people at all social levels.

ANIMALS

Some countries practice the custom of hanging ornaments around the necks of animals. In India, for example, camels are decorated with many items, such as colored cords threaded with glass beads, colored ribbons, gilt wires with shells, pendants, and small bells.

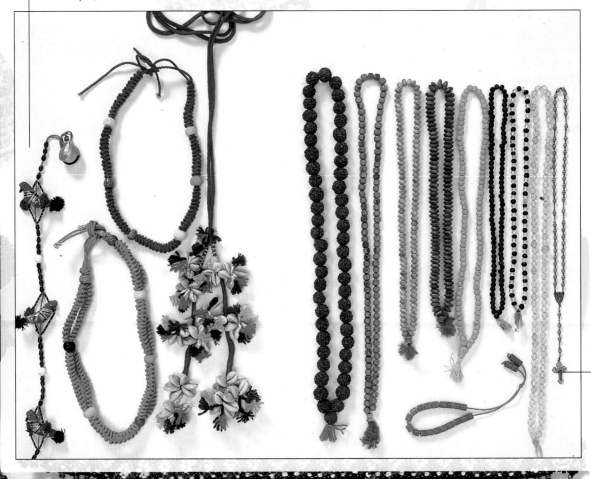

ROSARIES

The use of beads has not been limited to only ornamental functions, but also possesses a religious one as well. Rosaries, crowns of grains that are counted as they slip through one's fingers, can be found in many religions, such as Hinduism, Buddhism, Islam, and Christianity.

The Roman Catholic rosary, along with the crucifix that is attached to the beads, can be made be made of beads, gems, wood, and other materials.

The Hindu rosary is made up of 108 beads. The bead with the bow indicates the beginning and ending of prayer. It may be made of wood, but is often constructed with seeds—the Rudraksha nuts, which come from Java, being the most precious.

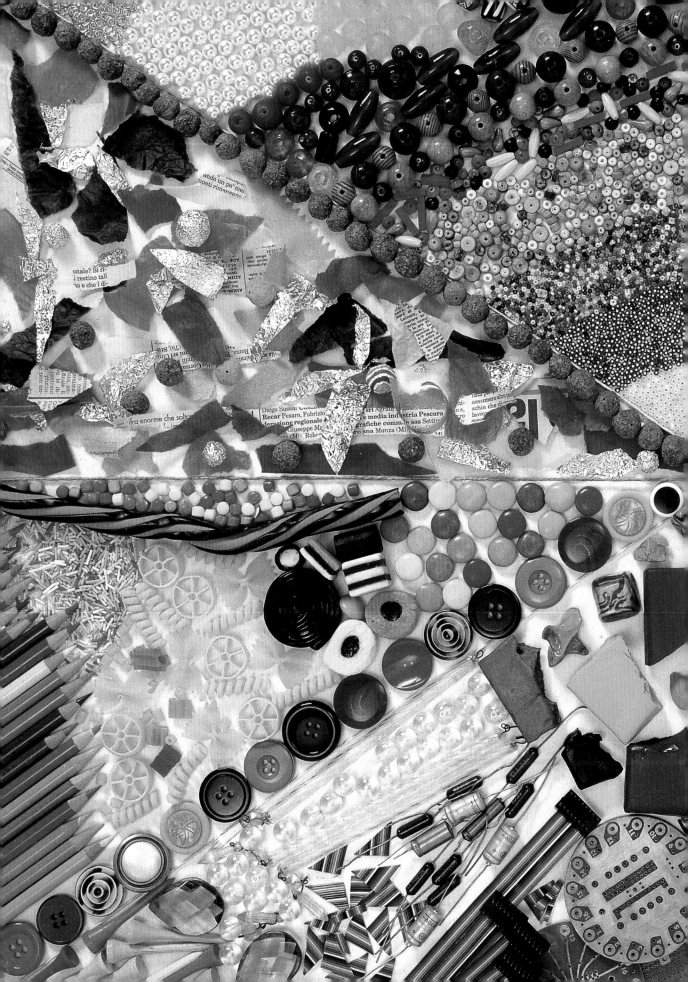

MATERIALS

TOOLS

NEEDLES
There are different kinds of needles for all types of wire, for making knots, and for making holes in seeds. Some of the more important needles you will want to start with are those:
– common for sewing
– with a small eye for beads
– with a big eye for cords
PLIERS
There are many kinds of pliers designed especially for jewelry making, but the most commonly used are:
– round nose, which are

used for making rings and jump rings with wire
– flat nose, which are used for bending wires
– chain nose, which are used for opening jump rings and tightening clasps
WIRE CUTTERS
These are used to cut wires and metal sheets cleanly:
– a metal cutter cuts large wires and metal sheets
– side cutting pliers are used to cut small wires
FILES
The market offers the following types:

– needle
– half-rounded
– fine-grained, which are used for filing cut wires
SCISSORS
It is best to use small-sized scissors with sharp, thin blades.
BEAD REAMER
This is useful for making holes in any type of material.
GLUES
Many different types of glue may be used according to the material they are to be applied to:
– white glue (PVA)
– epoxy

– adhesive silicone
PAINTS and VARNISHES
Whether transparent or opaque, paint is always useful for protecting jewelry made with easily damaged materials.
BRUSHES
You can use any kind of brush for painting, but flat brushes should be used for spreading varnish.
ADHESIVE TAPE
You will use adhesive tape to stiffen the end of cotton cords that need to be threaded without a needle.

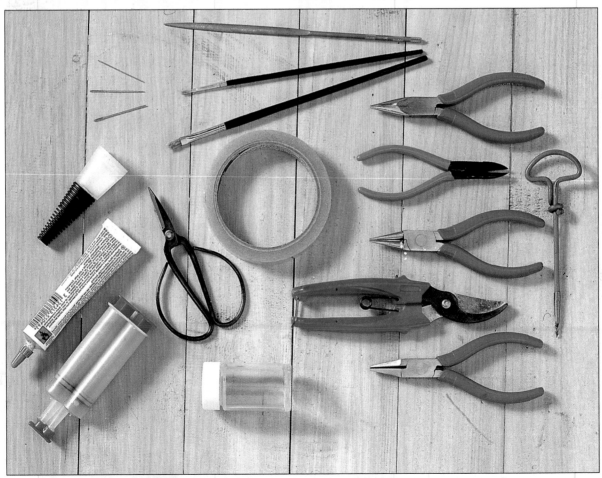

WIRES AND THREADS

NYLON WIRE
Use nylon wire with or without a needle; it is good for stringing heavy beads.

FISHING WIRE
This is very resistant.

SILK THREAD
This comes with one or two incorporated needles that range from number 0 to number 12. It is available in a wide range of colors.

COTTON THREAD
This thread, which is available in many colors and sizes, is suitable for stringing beads or for covering rubber tubing.

CORD
This is available in various colors and sizes and, with numerous knots, can be used for jewelry made with natural materials. If it is thin, it may be threaded. Wax cord allows beads to be strung more easily.

COTTON CORD
This is particularly useful when the hole is fairly large. It may be used with a needle or an end may be stiffened with adhesive tape, glue, or nail polish.

ELASTIC CORD
This is good for stringing bracelets. You do not need to use a clasp with elastic cord.

LEATHER CORD
This is available in various colors and is useful for stringing large beads, stones, and natural materials.

LACE
Lace is easy to use because the ends are already pre-cut, which makes them easy to insert into objects.

RIBBON
Ribbons are ideal for covering wooden rings and plastic tubes.

RUBBER CORD
This is good for all ornaments made of plastic materials.

MUSIC STEEL WIRE
The most common measurements are:
– $1/4$ inch for neck wires
– $1/8$ inch for hooks
– $1/16$ inch for stringing beads

BRASS WIRE
The most common measurements are:
– $1/4$ inch for neck wires
– $1/8$ inch for hooks

COPPER WIRE
The most common measurement for copper wire is $1/4$ inch, which is used for "caging".

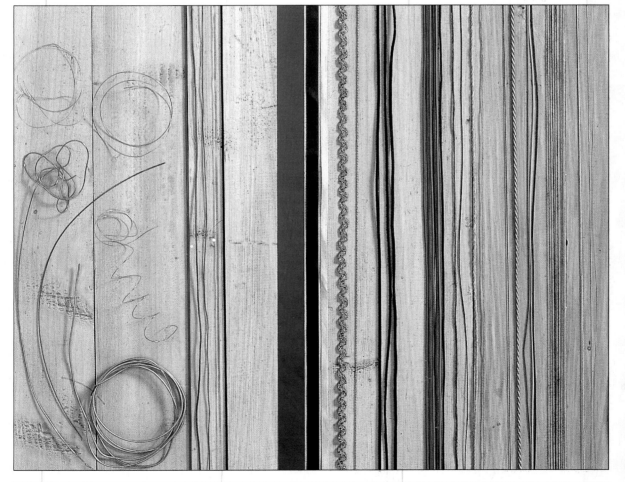

FINDINGS

Findings are small, metal elements used in making jewelry.

FINDINGS FOR NECKLACES AND BRACELETS

CLASPS
There are various types of clasps:
– Jump Rings are universal connector rings that are attached to the ends of wires or threads to fasten on either the jewelry itself or another type of clasp.
– Split Ring Clasps are essentially jump rings, but *have one ring that circles around itself. Use these for a more secure hold.*
– Spring Ring Clasps are rings that have an opening that can close.
– Lobster Claw Clasps function like spring ring clasps; they resemble a lobster's claw.
– Screw Clasps are made up of two parts that screw together. They have a metal ring at each end to which the thread or wire ends are knotted.
– Barrel Clasps are used to fasten necklaces with two wires or threads.

– Hook and Eye Clasps are made of two parts that hook onto each other.
GOLD AND SILVER WIRE
– These wires are tightly wound and are used to protect silk thread.
CORD CAPS
– Cord caps come in various shapes. They are placed at the ends of cords and threads.
CRIMP BEADS
– These are small clips used for blocking the thread when it has been knotted. There are various types available with or without holes.

SPACER BARS
– These are used for necklaces with many threads or cords. They help keep the rows apart.
NECK WIRE
– Neck wire is made of metal rings that have a hook for fastening.

FINDINGS FOR EARRINGS

The following are findings for pierced ears:
– Ear Wires are hooks of various shapes and lengths that have rings from which to hang the earrings.
– Srewback Earrings have a ring for attaching the earring and a butterfly fitting to tighten behind the ear lobe.
– Ear Posts have a flat base onto which the earring is glued.
The following are findings for non-pierced ears:
– Clip-On earrings come in various shapes and sizes.
– Ear Screws have a ring or a base for attaching the earring.

NAIL WIRES

Besides being employed for setting earrings, these are also useful for hooking pendants onto necklaces:
– Headpins are a $1/4$ inch thick and come in various lengths.
– Drop Wires are round earrings.

OTHER JEWELRY FINDINGS

BARRETTES

These have snap-clasps in iron, nickel, and silver and come in various lengths.

BROOCHES

These pins come in various shapes and sizes. They have a base to which any material can be glued on. They also have holes for attaching wires.

HAT PINS AND LAPEL PINS

These were created to decorate hats and coat lapels. They are often finished with a tapering bead.

RINGS

Jewelry can be mounted onto these ring bases.

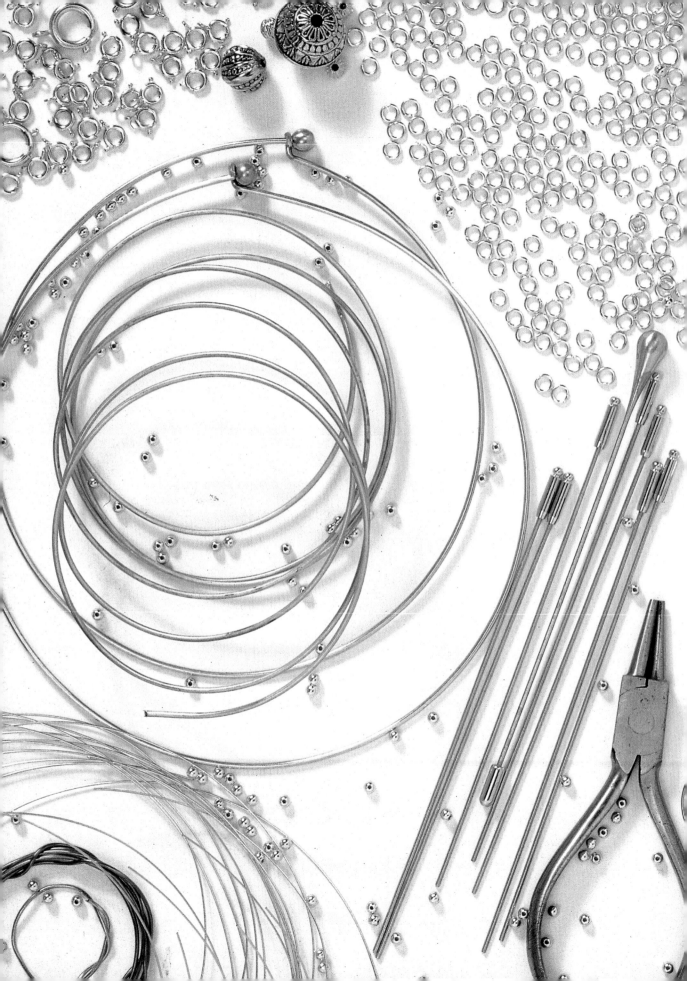

TECHNIQUES

THE PROJECT

When planning to make a necklace, it is best to first prepare a drawing so that you can decide on the shape and the length. If you would like to create a traditional type of necklace, the length of the wire will depend on many factors such as your height, the clothing that you intend to wear it with, and the style you want to express. Remember that the length of the wire must always be increased by 4 inches so that you will be able to make knots and attach the clasp. Here are some standard lengths that will serve as a reference:

- choker, length 14 inches
- neck wire, length 16 inches
- "princess", length 18 inches
- "matinée", length 24 inches
- "opera", length 35 inches
- "rope", length 44 inches.

When the length has been chosen, decide on what beads you would like to use. If you intend to string pearls or beads following the order of their sizes, use a wire with two needles. Begin at the center with the biggest bead and continue to string smaller beads (in a sequence) on both sides. You could, of course, use beads of the same size and separate them from each other with other smaller beads, using different colors or materials. If you do not have any small beads, knots will do fine for separating. Before you begin, spread out your sequence on a jewel tray; this will allow you to make any adjustments or changes. The necklace may be made with various wires of decreasing length—about 1¹/₂ inches less for each row. They can join into one wire at about halfway along the neck wire, or be kept separated by spacer bars along the whole length. The size and weight of the beads will determine both the type of wire to use and the shape of the necklace—with the weight placed in the center, it will take on a "V" shape; with weight evenly distributed, it will take on a more rounded shape. If you use music steel wire or brass wire as the supporting base, the necklace will have a circular shape. You can use these same techniques to make bracelets. The circumference of a bracelet varies according to the size of one's wrist, but it is usually between 6 and 7 inches.

STRINGING BEADS

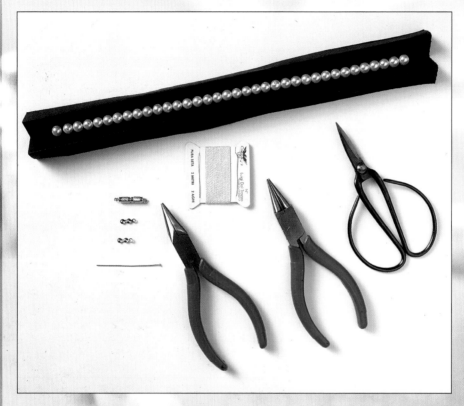

MATERIALS

39 INCHES OF SILK THREAD, NUMBER 9
44 PEARLS, ¼ INCH IN DIAMETER
2 CRIMP BEADS
1 SCREW CLASP
ROUND AND FLAT NOSE PLIERS
SCISSORS
CARDBOARD

MAKING A BEAD TRAY

Obtain some cardboard that is at least 12 x 5 inches, and fold it lengthwise in two.
Fold the two halves again lengthwise. You now should have an "M"-shaped tray onto which you can lay your pearls. You could make your tray the same length as your necklace or bracelet so that you will be able to estimate the exact number of pearls needed. Place them in order along the groove.

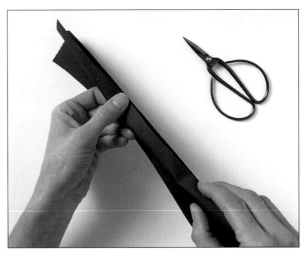

BEFORE STRINGING

A neckband of 15$\frac{1}{2}$ inches will need 44 pearls, $\frac{1}{4}$ inch in diameter.

Take a thread of white silk number 9 and thread the needle. Make a knot at the end opposite of the needle. Insert a crimp bead and slip it along the thread until you reach the knot. Place the knot into one of the crimp bead's hemispheres and then close with flat nose pliers. You will have a sphere containing the knot.

Let the end of the thread stick out—it will later be cut off when the necklace is finished.

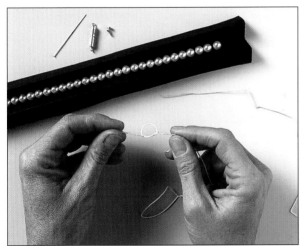

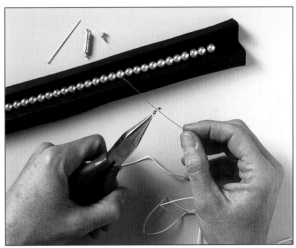

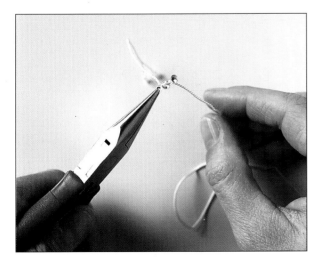

Insert the first pearl and slip it to the crimp bead.
Knot the thread and, keeping the knot loop wide, slip it
along to the pearl with the help of a needle.
Tighten the knot well.
Insert another pearl and make the same knot as before.

All the knots must be placed near the pearls to prevent
them from moving.
After stringing the last pearl, insert the crimp bead and
knot.

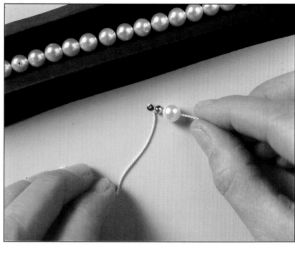

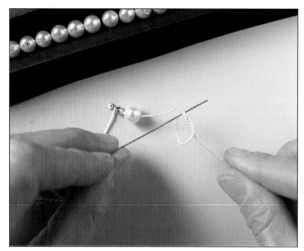

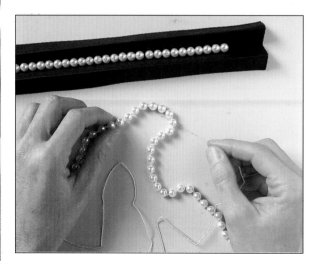

Close the crimp bead as before.

With scissors, cut off any threads that hang from the crimp bead.

At this point use a screw clasp to fasten the necklace.

Using two pliers, open the ring of the clasp, hook it onto the ring of the crimp bead, and then close it carefully with the flat nose pliers.

Your necklace is now ready to wear.

GOLD WIRE AND SCREW CLASP

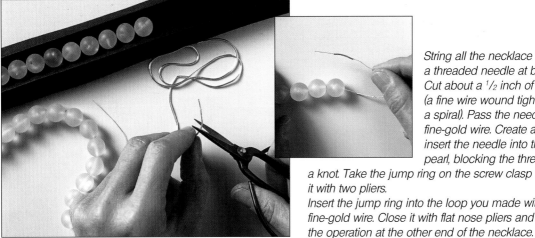

String all the necklace beads using a threaded needle at both ends. Cut about a $1/2$ inch of gold wire (a fine wire wound tightly into a spiral). Pass the needle inside the fine-gold wire. Create a loop and insert the needle into the last pearl, blocking the thread with a knot. Take the jump ring on the screw clasp and open it with two pliers.

Insert the jump ring into the loop you made with the fine-gold wire. Close it with flat nose pliers and repeat the operation at the other end of the necklace.

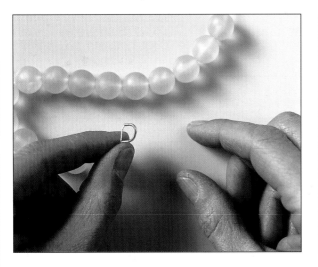

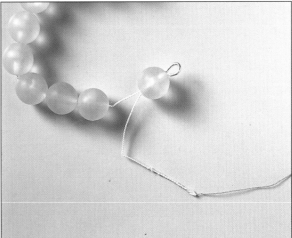

SOME TIPS FOR REAL PEARLS

Pearls, especially when of value (not artificial), need more attention than other precious stones.
Put them on only when you are already dressed so that they do not get caught in your clothing.
Perfumes and hair spray contain substances that can damage them. Saline and chlorine are harmful and
weaken the thread. Therefore, it is advisable to remove your pearls before taking a bath or shower.
Always clean pearls by polishing them with a cloth. The absence of light and air causes the surface pf pearls
to crack; so, they should be worn often to keep their luster intact.

PAPIER-MÂCHÉ

MAKING PAPIER-MÂCHÉ: WHAT TO DO

MATERIALS

PAPER (BROWN PAPER BAGS, NEWSPAPERS, EGG CARTONS, TISSUE PAPER, OR PAPER NAPKINS)

RUBBER GLOVES

STRAINER

BOWL

BLENDER

SMALL PLASTIC BAGS

POWDERED WALLPAPER PASTE

TABLESPOON

Tear the paper into small pieces and place them in water. Shred the paper pieces in the water and knead them into pulp. Use rubber gloves when doing this.

A blender can be used to get a perfectly smooth result. Place the pulp into a strainer and squeeze well to eliminate excess water—do not, however, dry it too much.

If the pulp is too much for your needs, keep it in an airtight plastic bag to keep it damp (freezing bags are ideal). If it is left out, the paste will become dry in about half an hour and be unusable.
To create papier-mâché, glue must now be added.
Powdered wallpaper paste is the best, but white glue (PVA) will do just as well.
Dissolve the powder carefully in water, following the instructions and measurements indicated on the package. Mix until the solution has a gel consistency.
Gradually add sufficient quantities to ensure a soft, elastic, and workable paste that is similar to bread dough. Knead well to eliminate all lumps.
Your papier-mâché is now ready to use.

In the lower right photo are some examples of papier-mâché made with different kinds of paper.

NECKLACE

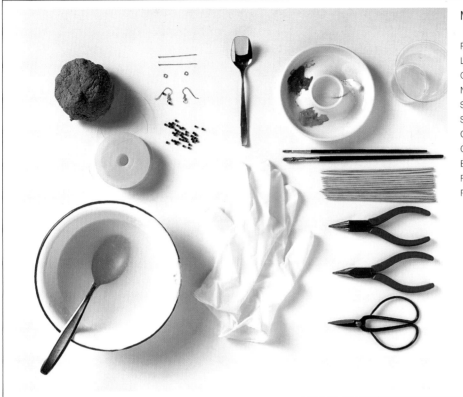

MATERIALS

PAPIER-MÂCHÉ
LONG TOOTHPICKS
GLUE
NYLON THREAD
SCISSORS
SPATULA OR TEASPOON
COLOR PAINTS AND BRUSHES
OPAQUE ACRYLIC VARNISH
BLACK BEADS
ROUND AND FLAT NOSE
PLIERS

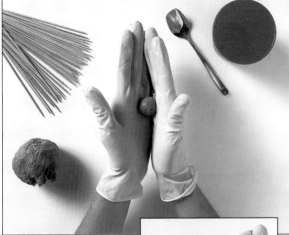

Take a small amount of papier-mâché and knead it into a small ball that is $1/2$ inch in diameter. Smooth the surface using a spatula or a teaspoon.

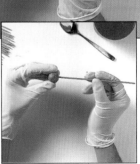

Insert a toothpick into the ball and rotate it delicately. Using the same amount of papier-mâché, make another small ball of the same previous size. Continue to make bigger balls so that you have two equally sized balls in each size. Make one huge ball for the center of the necklace. You will have a papier-mâché "pearl" necklace.

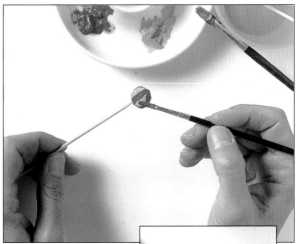

Let the balls dry for several days far from heat. Make sure that unsightly cracks do not appear; if they do, smooth the surface with a spoon.

Once the balls are dry, paint them by holding them with a long toothpick.

Since newspaper was used for the necklace shown, the papier-mâché looks dark. It is, therefore, advisable to spread a coat of a white primer before you paint them.

Decorate as desired with a fine brush.
Let the paint dry well every time you change the color. Finish with a light coat of an opaque acrylic varnish.

String the balls on the nylon thread, separating each one with a black bead. If your necklace is long enough you can do without a clasp and just knot the thread.

Here are some
examples of how a
necklace can be
fastened. Some of
the clasps are made
of papier-mâché.

NECKLACE AND EARRINGS

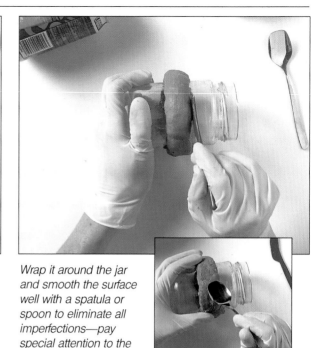

NECKLACE – Take a glass jar or a tin can with a circumference of about 2 inches. Mold a small amount of papier-mâché into a long, narrow shape.

Wrap it around the jar and smooth the surface well with a spatula or spoon to eliminate all imperfections—pay special attention to the edges.

Let the necklace dry for several days and then slide it delicately off the jar.

The necklace may be painted with paint or Indian ink. You could even add the color directly to the papier-mâché. You could also keep the original color of the papier-mâché, particularly if it is made of cardboard or brown wrapping paper, and decorate it by scorching various areas with the tip of a welder.

When the work is finished, spread a coat of a transparent varnish to protect the necklace and to give it a glossy look.

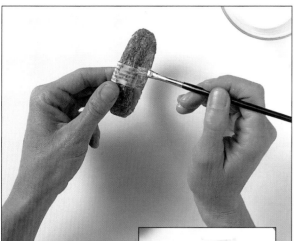

NECKLACE – Take a papier-
mâché necklace and
cover it with newspaper
that has been cut into
small strips. Dissolve
1 tablespoon of water to
5 tablespoons of glue
and coat the necklace
with a brush, moistening
the strips carefully with the mixture.

You could also cut lager
sized strips of paper and
glue them on at the end
of the work to enrich the
decoration. Let dry.
Spread a coat of a
transparent-glossy acrylic
varnish.

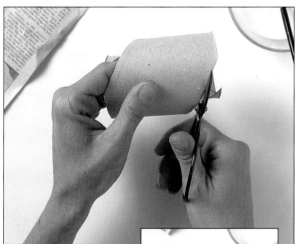

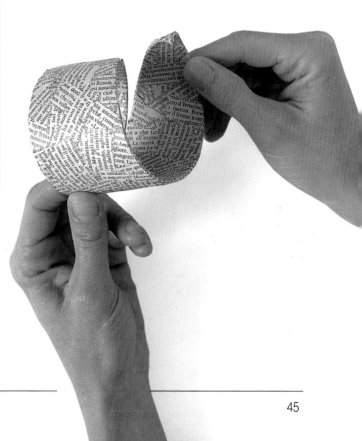

NECKLACE – Take the
cardboard that is in a roll
of toilet paper.
Cut it along the joining
until it is completely open.
Trim off some edges to
give it a more attractive
shape. Cut the newspaper
into small pieces and
cover the cardboard with them, using a brush dipped in
water and glue. When dry, coat with a protective varnish.

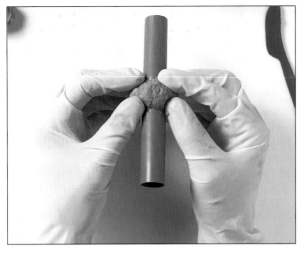

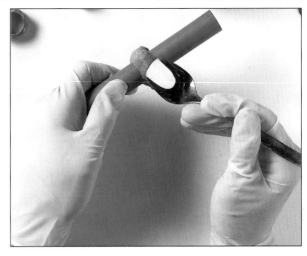

Ring – To make a ring, it is essential to have a stiff support to work the papier-mâché on. Choose a tube of the same circumference as your finger and work the papier-mâché into a long, narrow shape.

Wrap it around the tube and smooth it, trying to give the ring the desired shape. Remember that the thinner part must be turned towards your palm. Leave to dry color as wished and proteet the ring with a coat of varnish.

Barrette – Use your own imagination with geometrical and fancy shapes, but if you run out of ideas, try using cookie cutters. Fill them with papier-mâché. Press the papier-mâché firmly with your fingers and smooth with a spoon.

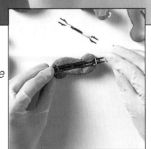

Open the metal barrette and take out the central piece. Carefully pry out the papier-mâché from the mold and warp it around the metal base of the barrette.

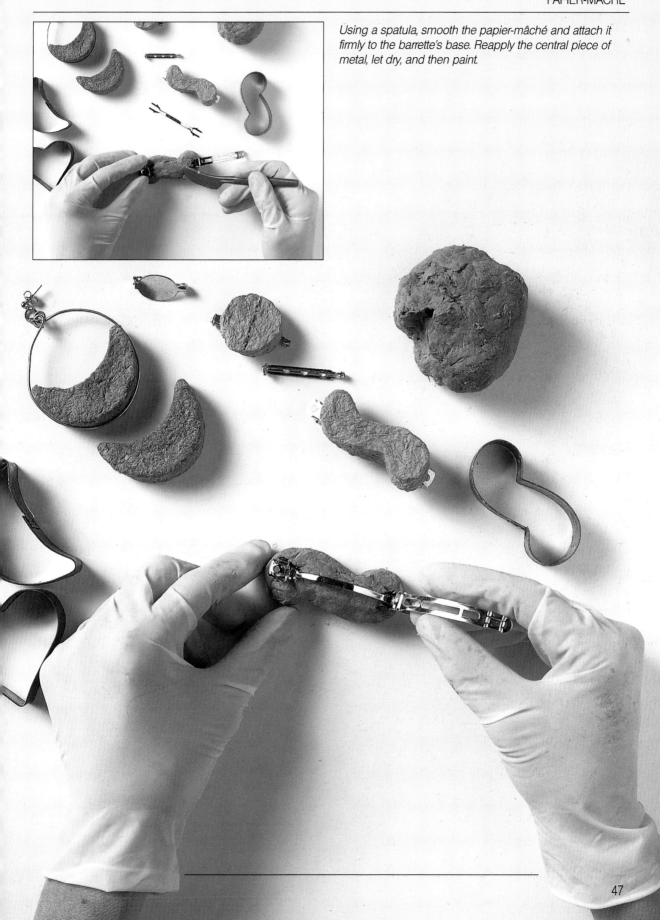

Using a spatula, smooth the papier-mâché and attach it firmly to the barrette's base. Reapply the central piece of metal, let dry, and then paint.

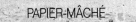

Here are some exotic and delightful necklaces made with papier-mâché balls. In the first example the "pearls" are painted with Indian ink (a fine paintbrush was used). In the second, the natural color of papier-mâché was kept.

Instead of papier-mâché balls, one necklace here has small parallelepipeds separated by red wood beads. The other has little cylinders painted with Indian ink on the sides and separated by pinecone shells.

In the necklace and bracelet shown here, the papier-mâché was worked without being smoothed—the balls are wrinkled and irregular.

In this bracelet gold paint was spread with a dry brush to highlight the uneven surface.

The three rows of this necklace are kept apart by a spacer bar, also made of papier-mâché. Three holes were bored in it, and the threads were joined into one beyond the spacer bar.

Let your imagination run wild and you can make papier-mâché ornaments of all shapes and colors.

These irregular balls, the color of the paper and lightly varnished to shield against water, can be strung on neck wire or knotted on a thin cord.

TINFOIL NECKLACE

MATERIALS

TINFOIL
THREAD
SPRING RING CLASP
2 CRIMP BEADS
3 JUMP RINGS
SCISSORS
ROUND AND FLAT NOSE
PLIERS
SEWING NEEDLE
2 EYE NEEDLES
2 EAR SCREWS

Take some tinfoil and wrinkle it a little.
Cut pairs of squares. Start at $1/8$ inch and increase the size by increments of $1/2$ inch until you reach 4 inches.
Roll the tinfoil into round balls.
Place the tinfoil "pearls" in a pearl tray in their ascending order of size.

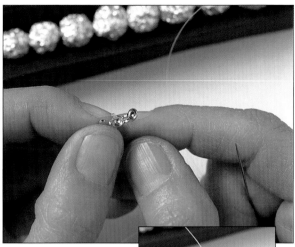

Pierce all the pearls
with a needle.
Take the thread,
preferably nylon,
and make a knot at
one end.

Insert a silver colored
crimp bead and place
the knot in it with pliers.

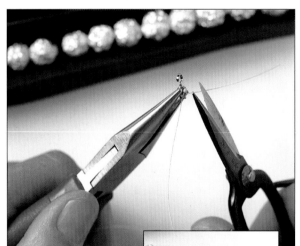

Cut the excess thread
with scissors.
String the pearls in their
ascending order.

When finished, block the
thread again with a
crimp bead and attach
the spring ring clasp.

EARRINGS – Use two tinfoil pearls of different sizes for each earring. Pierce the earrings with the eye needles. Take a silver colored eye needle and insert it. With round nose pliers, make a loop with the excess wire.

Fasten on the jump rings and insert the ear screws.

JEWELRY MADE WITH NATURAL MATERIALS

PINECONE NECKLACE

MATERIALS

1 LARGE PINECONE
COLORED WOODEN BEADS
BEAD REAMER
ROUND AND FLAT NOSE
PLIERS
SCISSORS
SIDE CUTTING PLIERS
BLACK WAX CORD
FINE WIRE (BRASS), 1/8-INCH THICK
1 LARGE WOODEN BEAD
OPAQUE VINYL VARNISH
2 EAR WIRES
2 JUMP RINGS

Strip about twenty pinecone shells, which contain its seeds, from a dry pinecone. With a bead reamer, make a small hole in the narrowest part of each shell. Cut twenty pieces that are about 3/4-inch long from the brass wire.

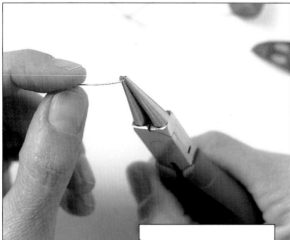

Take a piece of the brass wire, make a small loop with the round nose pliers, and insert the wire into the hole of the pine shells.

Take a piece of the brass wire, make a small loop with the round nose pliers, and insert the wire into the hole of the pine shells.

With the black wax cord, string on a ring and two different-colored beads. Repeat this operation eight times.

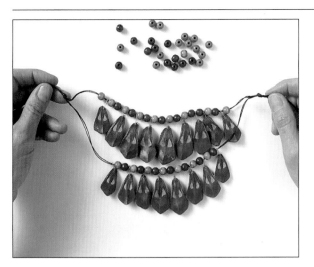

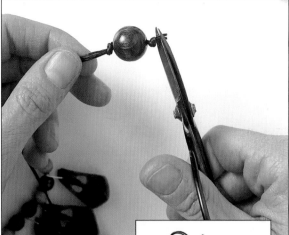

Take some more wax cord and string a wooden bead. Continue this sequence nine times.
Lay the two rows out flat and knot them together so that they barely overlap.

A big wooden bead could be fastened. String it at one end of the thread and block it with two knots, one on each side. Make a loop at the other end and block it with a knot. To protect the shells, you can finish with a coat of an opaque acrylic varnish.

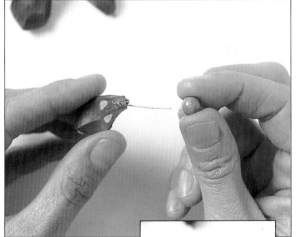

EARRINGS – Take a shell for each earring and pierce it on top with the bead reamer. Insert a piece of brass wire and fasten with a jump ring.

Insert the piece of metal into the holes of the two wooden beads and close with another jump ring. Attach an ear wire of the same metal. Repeat the process for the other earring.

Dried fruit and big and small seeds that are both round and tapering are used to make these necklaces. In some of the necklaces, small, colored beads were used to separate these elements.

The large red seeds of the Cycas revoluta, *together with the small seeds of the medlar, are strung together on fine brass wire that is attached to a neck wire, also made of brass but thicker.*

This simple necklace was made with chili peppers strung together.

Here is a necklace that is made of carob pods and other large flat pods. Small fragments of gilt wire attach the various pieces, leaving the jump ring barely visible.

A large Mexican bean and cones from the Terra del Fuego, together with fish vertebrae and black beads, were used to make this simple necklace.

When the cones of the cypress dry, they separate from the branches, take on a brown color, and open, creating a sphere. In this necklace wooden beads were added to separate the cones from each other.

Here, the large seeds of the South American walnut were alternated with glass beads and colored disks. A cord acts as a support for the necklace.

This original three-row necklace is made of light and dark dried beans.

Acorns, nutshells, and medlar seeds have been strung on three rows, which were then united by a spacer bar made of papier-mâché.

SHELL NECKLACE

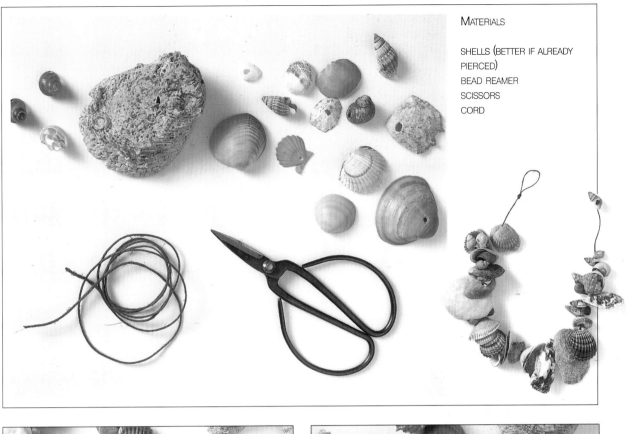

MATERIALS

SHELLS (BETTER IF ALREADY
PIERCED)
BEAD REAMER
SCISSORS
CORD

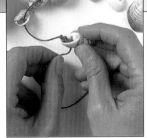

Obtain some shells.
If you are lucky some will
already have holes in
them. If not, pierce the
shells with a bead
reamer or a drill. String
them on a piece of cord
and, if necessary, make
knots to keep them
separated.

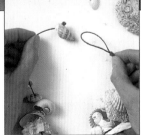

Close with a shell tied to
one end of the cord and
block with two knots, one
on each side. Make a
loop at the other end of
the cord that is big
enough for the shell to
pass through.

A long piece of cord was used to string these small, twisted shells. The necklace may also be worn by wrapping two rows around the neck.

A single, eye-catching shell is the center of attention in this easily made necklace, and is accompanied by glass beads and cylinders of semi-precious stones.

Large, smooth white shells are strung on a colored cord and are alternated with flower petals, citrus fruit peels, and dry leaves on this necklace.

Strung together here are pumice stones of various sizes that are alternated with seeds.

Mediterranean seeds, together with smooth and twisted branches and clusters of shells, are the elements that were used in the two necklaces in the center.

The earrings shown here were created with attractive pieces of wood and simple pierced shells. A small seed provides the decorative element. A simple ear wire is attached to them.

Pieces of smooth, twisted wood, polished by the movement of the sea and sand, can easily be found on the beach and turned into beautiful necklaces.

ORANGE PEELS AND ALMONDS

MATERIALS

ORANGE PEELS
ALMONDS (WITH THEIR
SHELLS)
BEAD REAMER
SIDE CUTTING PLIERS
ROUND NOSE PLIERS
16 INCHES OF MUSIC STEEL
WIRE, 1/4-INCH THICK
7 INCHES OF MUSIC STEEL
WIRE, 1/8-INCH THICK

Cut the orange peel into eight
segments. Leave them to
desiccate in a dry place between
two paper towels or newspaper
with a weight on top (to prevent
the peels from buckling).
Take nine almonds and pierce
the center of the shells with a
bead reamer.
Pierce the eight pieces of orange
peels at one end.

Cut ⁷/₈-inch long strips from the ¹/₈-inch thick music steel wire with side cutting pliers. Using round nose pliers, make a small ring at one end of each piece.

Insert a strip of the music steel wire into one of the orange peel pieces. Bend the inserted end with pliers to obtain a small ring. Repeat this operation with all of the orange peels.

Cut 16 inches of the music steel wire with side cutting pliers. String on the almonds and the orange peels.

With the round nose pliers, make the necklace clasp by creating a ring at one end and a hook at the other.

Seeds, shells, and even fishing floats make up the components of this necklace, which is finished off with a sequence of red seeds.

These feathers, rice grains, and pasta rings strung on a black-colored cord recall the ornaments of the North American Indian tribes.

An assortment of petals, leaves, and flowers on fine wire decorates this neck wire, which suggests the fragrances of spring.

MOSAIC NECKLACE

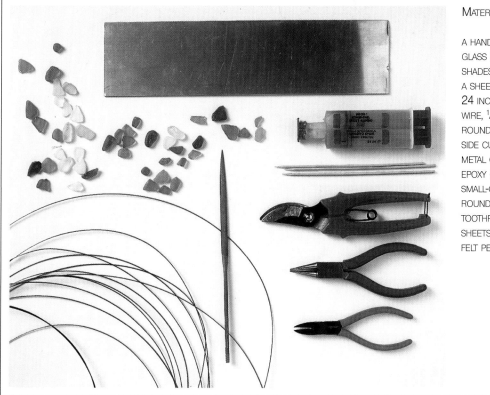

MATERIALS

A HANDFUL OF SMALL SEA
GLASS PIECES IN VARIOUS
SHADES OF GREEN
A SHEET OF ALUMINUM
24 INCHES OF MUSIC STEEL
WIRE, 1/4-INCH THICK
ROUND NOSE PLIERS
SIDE CUTTING PLIERS
METAL CUTTER
EPOXY GLUE
SMALL-GRAINED SEMI-
ROUNDED NEEDLE FILE
TOOTHPICKS
SHEETS OF PAPER
FELT PEN

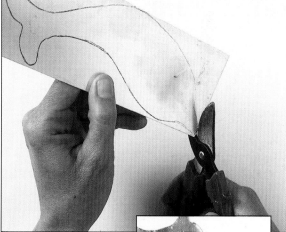

Draw a design of your choice on a sheet of paper. It could be a regular geometric shape, an abstract one, or a form inspired by nature. We chose a dolphin for this necklace. Cut out the shape and place it on a sheet of aluminum (if you do not have aluminum, use another smooth, stiff material). Mark the outline on the aluminum sheet with a felt pen.

With a metal cutter, cut out the shape and file all around the edges. Pierce a hole at the two ends to attach the hooks or rings. Take some pieces of smooth glass and lay them onto the cutout shape, choosing colors ranging from white to dark green. Try to cover the whole area of the shape, leaving small spaces between the glass pieces.

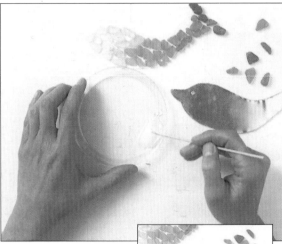

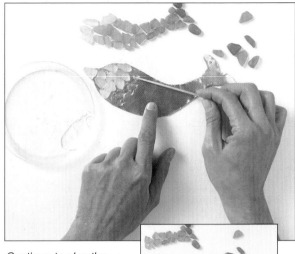

With a toothpick spread a little bit of glue on one part of the aluminum shape and start gluing on the glass pieces in order, (in this case, beginning with the head).

Continue to glue the glass pieces. When finished, place a weight on top to keep your mosaic under pressure.

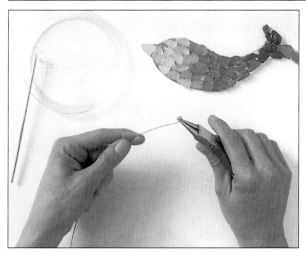

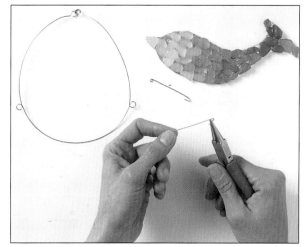

Take some music steel wire and cut two 2 1/2-inch long strips.
With another piece of wire, form a necklace. File the ends and make a ring at one end and a hook at the other for the clasp. Shape two rings with the pliers at the front of the necklace at about 7 inches from each other.

Attach one end of a piece of steel wire to a ring on the necklace. Bend the other to form a hook, which will pass through the hole made in the metal shape.
Repeat this operation on the other side.

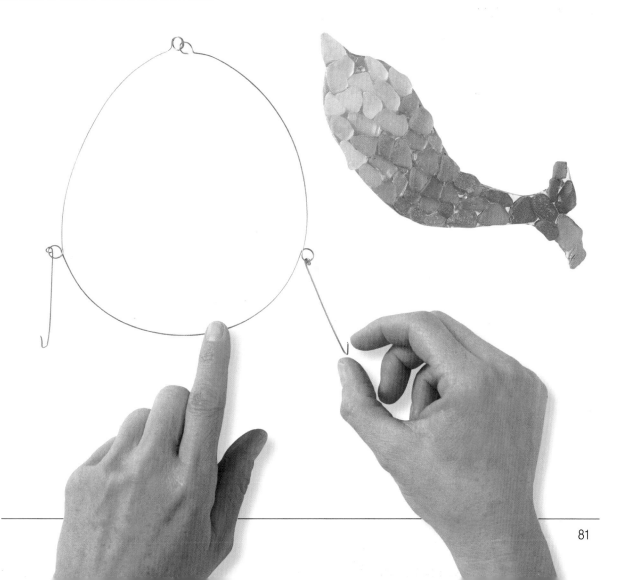

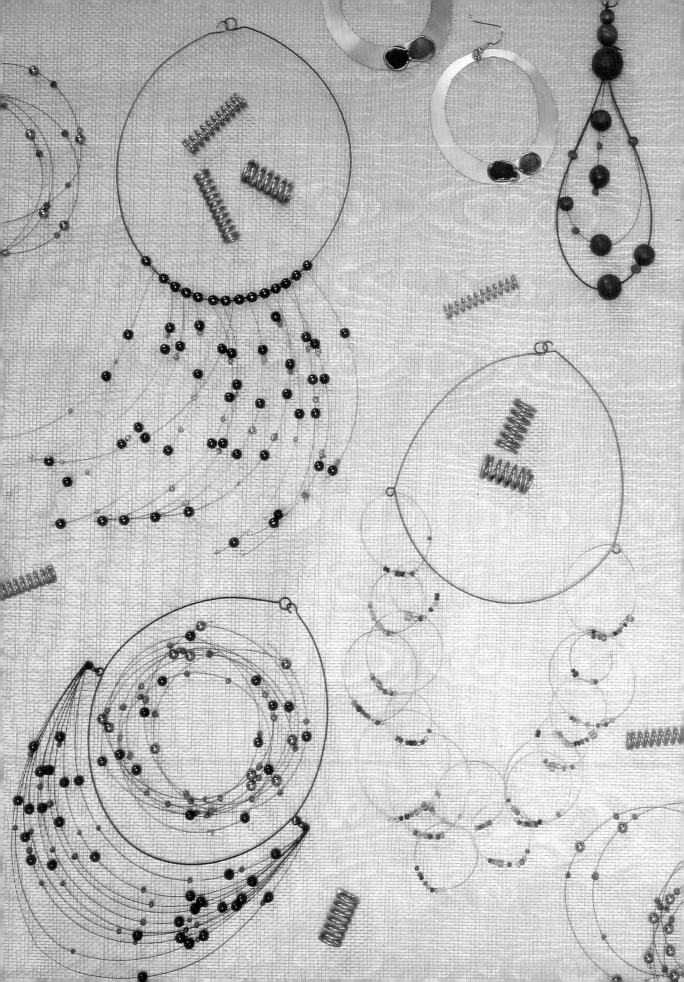

USING METALS

PENDANT NECKLACE

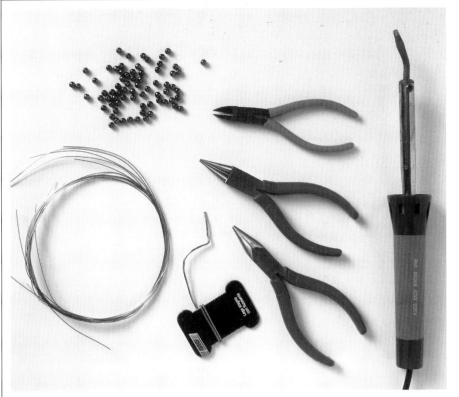

MATERIALS

METAL BEADS
16 INCHES OF MUSIC STEEL WIRE, 1/4-INCH THICK
MUSIC STEEL WIRE, 1/8-INCH THICK
SOLDERING IRON
SOLDER
ROUND AND FLAT NOSE PLIERS
SIDE CUTTING PLIERS
FILE

Take the 1/8-inch thick music steel wire and cut thirteen 6-inch long strips. Take the 16-inch long music steel wire and turn it into a neck wire. With the pliers, make a ring at one end. Make a small ring at each end of the thirteen wire strips. String a metal bead on each strip.

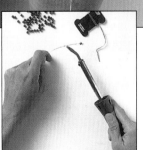

With a soldering iron, melt a drop of solder and attach it to the music steel wire at about 1 1/4 inch from the end.

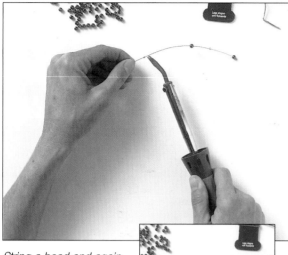

String a bead and again attach a drop of solder. Continue like this to the end. Close the opposite end of the wire with a small ring to prevent the beads from falling off.

Attach the pendant to the neck wire. Repeat this process for the other twelve strips, separating each one with a bead.

Close the neck wire by making a hook with pliers.

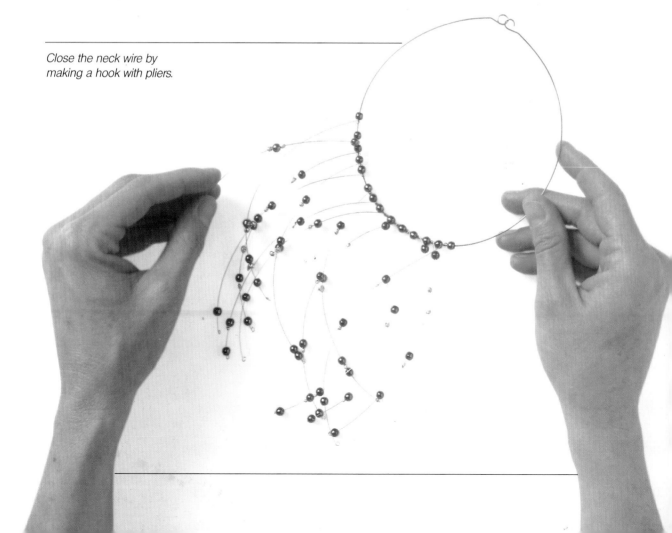

With brass, copper, or steel wires, you can enclose stones, terracotta fragments, marbles, or colored sea glass. When making rings, wrap the wire around a base with the same dimensions as your finger. Attach the stone you intend to use, and wrap it around until it remains firm. With the same technique you can make a barrette. Attach the wire to a clip and then wrap three smooth, round stones with copper wire.

The copper wire could also be strung with glass beads and then attached to a clip.

Colored wooden beads and tiny glass beads make up the pendants shown on the necklaces and bracelets on the opposite page. The base is made of music steel wire with a varying thickness.

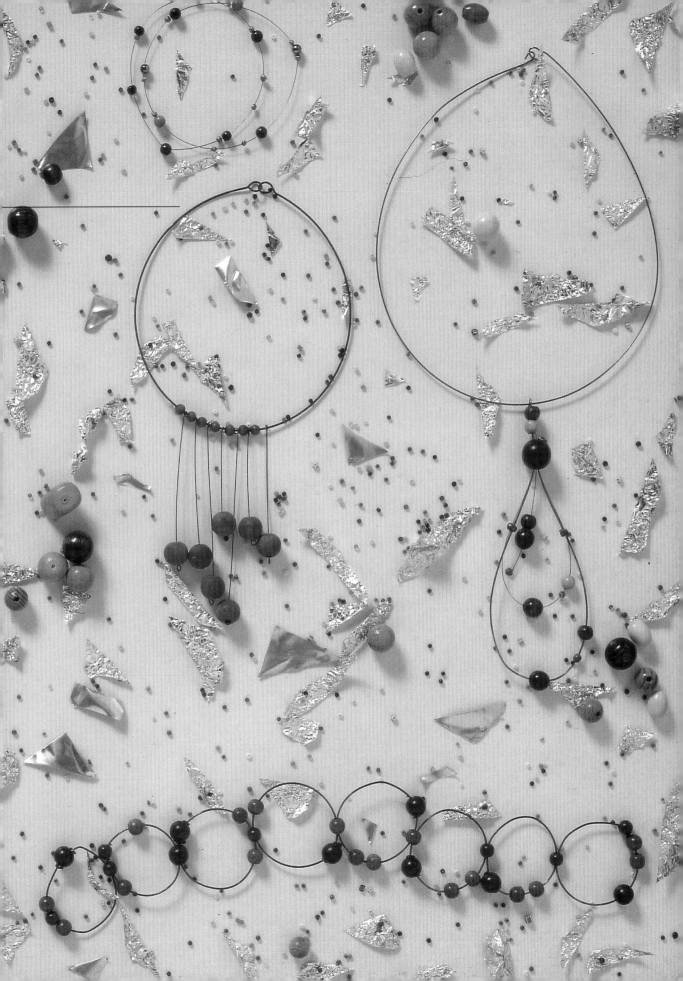

BRASS NECKLACE

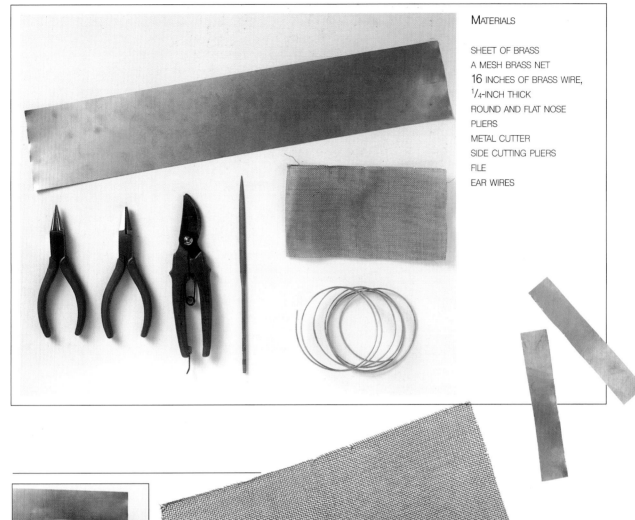

MATERIALS

SHEET OF BRASS
A MESH BRASS NET
16 INCHES OF BRASS WIRE,
$1/4$-INCH THICK
ROUND AND FLAT NOSE
PLIERS
METAL CUTTER
SIDE CUTTING PLIERS
FILE
EAR WIRES

With the metal cutter, cut two 3 x $1/2$ inch rectangles and two $3/4$ x $3/4$ inch squares from the sheet of brass. From the brass net, cut a 2 x 1 inch rectangle and two $3/4$ x $3/4$ inch squares.

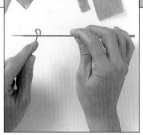

With pliers, bend the brass wire to make a neck wire. Create a small ring at one end and a hook at the other for the clasp. Carefully file the cut ends.

Take the brass net rectangle and fold back the short side over the center of the neck wire. Tighten it with flat nose pliers. Attach the two brass rectangles onto the sides of the brass net rectangle and twist them around the wire.

Twist the two brass net squares around the neck wire to form two triangles. Repeat the same operation with the brass squares, making them slightly overlap the brass net squares. Tighten well with pliers so that all the elements are firmly in position.

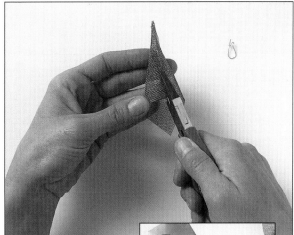

EARRINGS − With the metal side cutting pliers, cut two 3 x 3 1/2 inch rectangles from the brass net, each one will be an earring. Roll the rectangles into cones.

Lightly press the brass net with pliers to keep the desired shape. Cut two half-moon shapes from a sheet of brass.

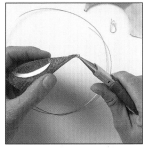

Attach the half-moons by sticking the tips in the mesh. Fasten on a ring to the top of the cone and insert an ear wire.

These four triangles, made from two different hammered metals, were joined together in pairs with small rings.

Copper and brass are the raw materials used in these ornaments. Metal sheets cut into geometrical shapes and fine-meshed metal nets were bent, assembled, and beaten in different ways and patterns.

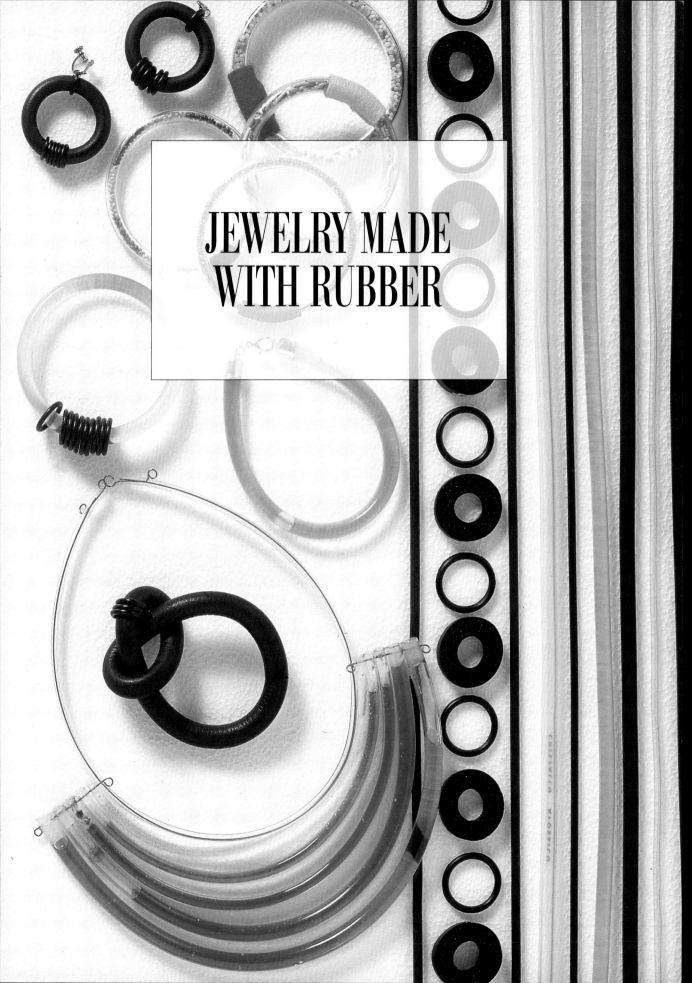

JEWELRY MADE WITH RUBBER

RUBBER NECKLACE

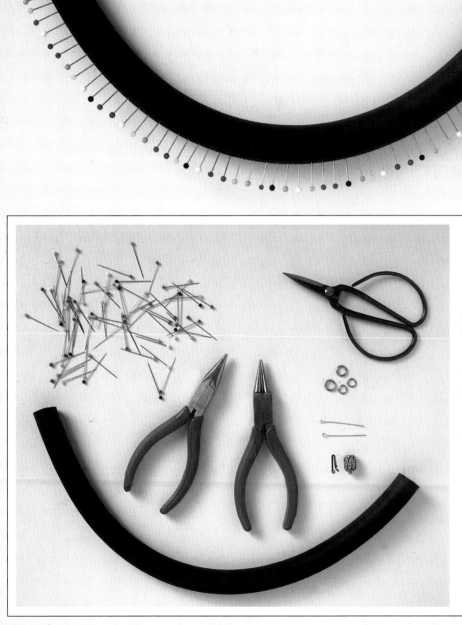

MATERIALS

PINS WITH COLORED GLASS
HEADS
2 EYE NEEDLES
16-INCH LONG PIECE OF
SOLID RUBBER, $3/4$-INCH THICK
SCISSORS
ROUND AND FLAT NOSE
PLIERS
4 JUMP RINGS (2 BIG AND 2
SMALL)
BARREL CLASP
$1/4$-INCH THICK RUBBER TUBE
GLUE

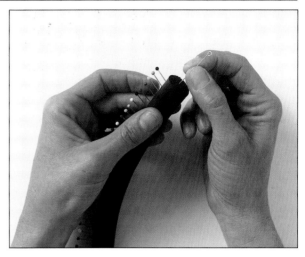

Take the 16 inch rubber tube and stretch it out on the table. Stick the pins ⅛ inch from each other.

Make sure that each pin sticks out about ¼ inch. To close the necklace, insert an eye needle into the center of the tube's end.

Attach a jump ring to one end and a barrel clasp to the other.

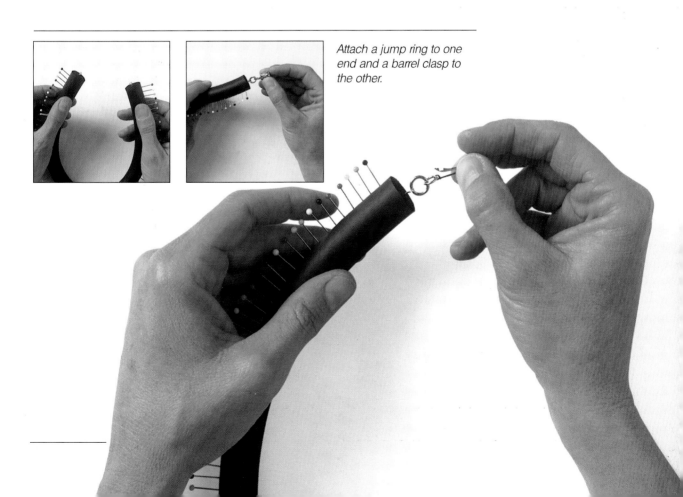

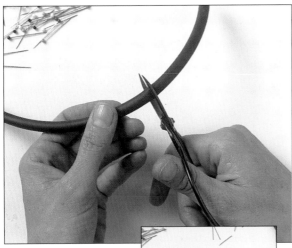

EARRINGS – With the same technique, earrings can be made by using a ¼-inch thick rubber tube. Cut a 4-inch long piece for each earring. Insert the pins after having broken them in half.

Glue the two ends of the rubber tube together.

Hold them firmly together for a few minutes. Insert an eye needle that is shorter than the tube piece and attach it to an ear wire.

To make earrings in the same style as the necklace, take a 6-inch long piece of rubber, ¼-inch thick, and make a knot. Glue a jump ring the back.

Solid rubber is the basic element for the examples shown here. It is soft to the touch, easy to cut, and easy to knot. Glass beads have been used as the decorative element in the necklace with several rows, whose trimmings, also in rubber, are of various sizes.

SPRING COIL NECKLACE

Here is another earring made from the same type of rubber tubing that was used for the necklace. Cut a 3½-inch long piece and make a knot at the end. Insert a 1 x ½-inch spring coil. Make a metal hook to attach the jump ring and ear screw on.

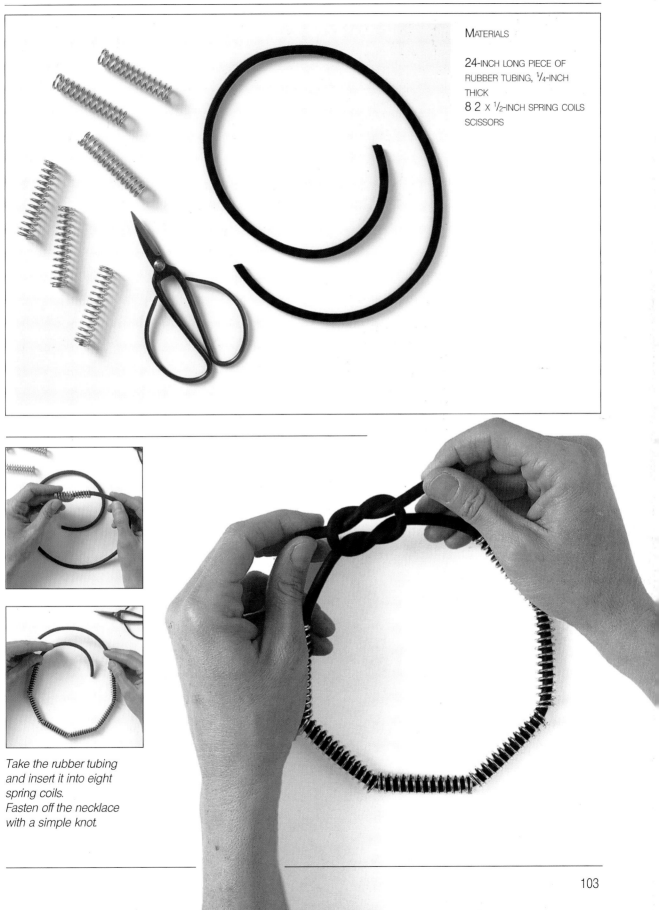

MATERIALS

24-INCH LONG PIECE OF
RUBBER TUBING, ¼-INCH
THICK
8 2 x ½-INCH SPRING COILS
SCISSORS

*Take the rubber tubing
and insert it into eight
spring coils.
Fasten off the necklace
with a simple knot.*

BRIGHTLY-COLORED NECKLACE

A HANDFUL OF SMALL SEEDS
MIXED WITH CAKE
DECORATIONS
18-INCH LONG PIECE OF
TRANSPARENT RUBBER
TUBING, 1/4-INCH THICK
ADHESIVE TAPE
2 CORD CAPS WITH CLASPS
SCISSORS
ROUND NOSE PLIERS
GLUE

Cut the transparent rubber tubing.

Close one end of the rubber tubing with adhesive tape.

Pour some seeds into the palm of your hand and slip them into the tube through the open end.
Bang the end of the tube on the table now and then to allow the seeds to tightly pack.

Seal off the other end with adhesive tape. Place a drop of glue inside both cord caps and insert them onto both ends.

All of these ornaments are made from pieces of transparent rubber tubing. Some are filled with colored beads, others with seeds or sparkles, and still others with confectionery. Attractive effects can also be achieved by using water colored with food coloring. When making these models, the ends were glued.

COLORED TUBING

For the earrings, string small
pieces of colored tubing
onto an eye needle. On one
end, create a ring and attach
a jump ring and ear screw.

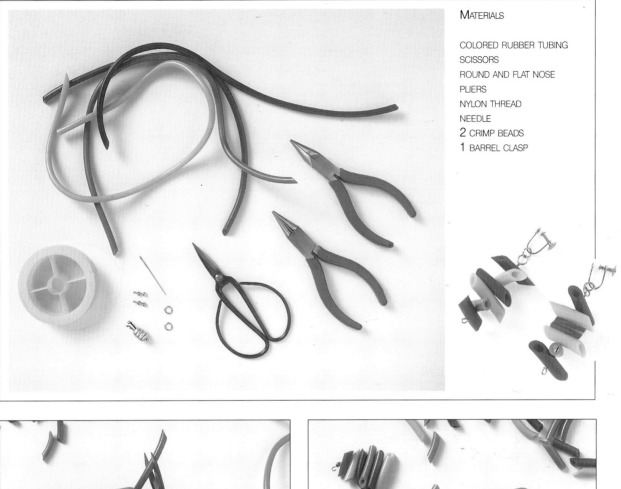

MATERIALS

COLORED RUBBER TUBING
SCISSORS
ROUND AND FLAT NOSE
PLIERS
NYLON THREAD
NEEDLE
2 CRIMP BEADS
1 BARREL CLASP

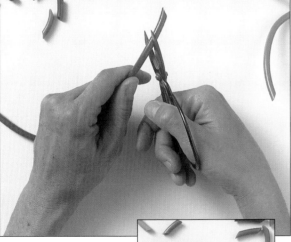

Take rubber tubing of four different colors, and cut them slantwise into 1¼-inch long pieces. With the nylon thread and a needle, pierce each piece at about half of its length.

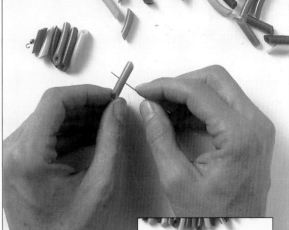

Insert a crimp bead and proceed until you reach about 27 inches. Alternate the four colors. Attach a barrel clasp with pliers.

JEWELRY
DECORATIONS

NECKLACE WITH FELT STRIPS

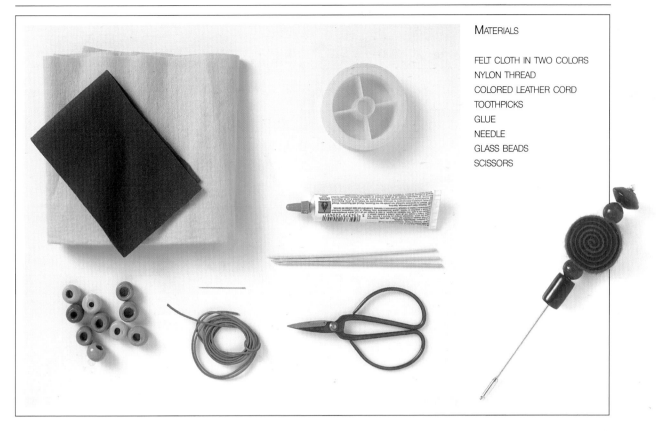

MATERIALS

FELT CLOTH IN TWO COLORS
NYLON THREAD
COLORED LEATHER CORD
TOOTHPICKS
GLUE
NEEDLE
GLASS BEADS
SCISSORS

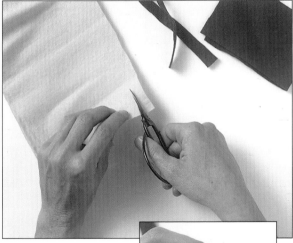

Cut two felt cloths into two 11 x ½-inch strips. Overlap them, keeping their edges together. Wrap them around a toothpick.

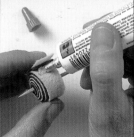

Make sure you evenly wrap them so that the two colors show in the spiral.
When you have finished this delicate operation, glue the ends of the strips down, being careful that the outer piece slightly overlaps and covers the inner piece.

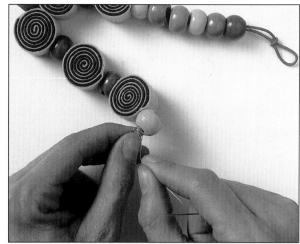

Using a needle and the nylon thread, string large glass beads. Begin with six. Then, insert the rolls of cloth, separated by other glass beads. Finish with six large glass beads.

With a colored leather cord knotted to the nylon thread, string again just the six initial and the six final glass beads.

For the clasp, you could use a roll made with some felt cloth in one of the colors with a loop at the other end.

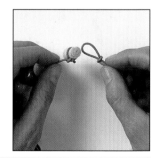

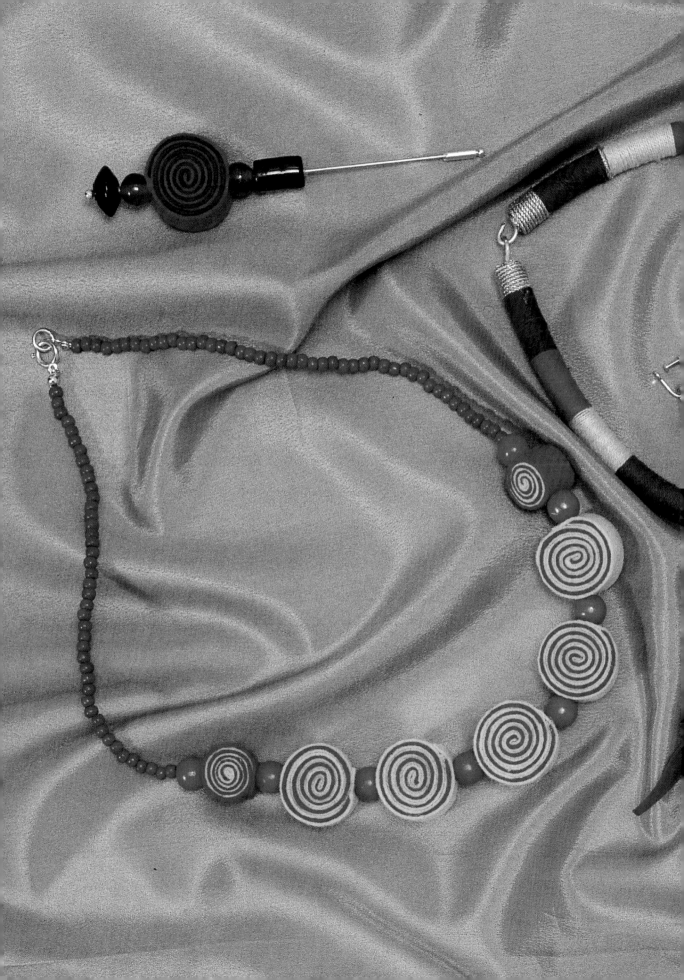

BRACELETS AND NECKLACES MADE WITH CORD

This necklace is made of silk cords of many colors that are twisted together and held at the ends by wrapped brass wire to which a clasp was then attached.

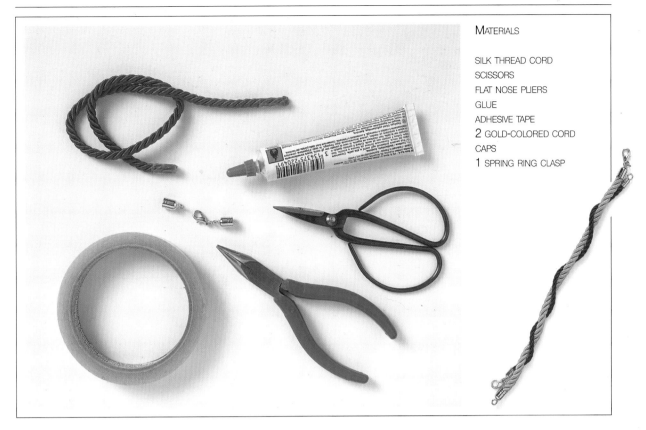

MATERIALS

SILK THREAD CORD
SCISSORS
FLAT NOSE PLIERS
GLUE
ADHESIVE TAPE
2 GOLD-COLORED CORD
CAPS
1 SPRING RING CLASP

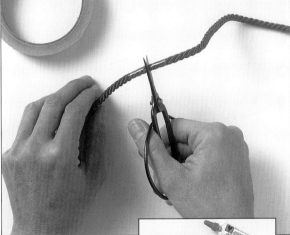

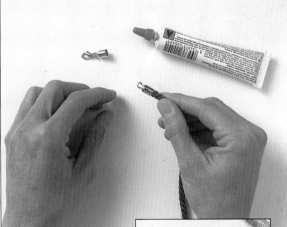

Take some cord made of twisted silk threads. Measure 6 inches in length and, at that point, wrap the cord with a piece of adhesive tape to prevent it from fraying before and after cutting. Take two gold-colored cord caps and squeeze a drop of glue into each one. Insert the two ends of the cord.

You could also tighten the metal with flat nose pliers. Attach a spring ring clasp.

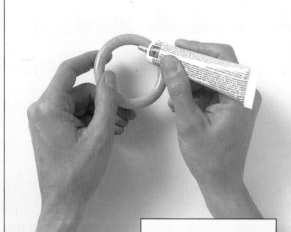

EARRINGS – Take a pair of ordinary wooden curtain rings.
Cover each ring with colored satin ribbon. Glue the ribbon at the beginning and at the end of the rings.

Wrap the whole surface around once more with silver trimming.

With some fine wire, make two or three turns around the earring and make a little loop. Attach a jump ring and the clasp.

Here is a striking necklace made with rubber tubing, which has been covered with various-colored silk threads. A gold thread was also applied at various places as well. Gold thread adorns the two ends, to which the clasp was added.

POLYMER CLAY

POLYMER CLAY

Cernit, Fimo, Formello, Sculpey III, and Prima are polymer clays that are excellent to work with. The vast range of colors available is sufficient to satisfy all of your needs. Attractive marble effects can be obtained by mixing various colors together. The clay can be exposed to the air; although it is a good idea to wrap it in plastic wrap once it is taken out. The clay is, however, sensitive to heat. It becomes softer as the temperature rises and harder as it falls. If baked in the oven at 212° F-248° F or boiled in water, polymer clay hardens and becomes resistant to the heat, cold, dampness, and water. To boil this material, place the beads you have made in a pot of cold water. Heat to 212° F and let them boil for five minutes. This technique, however, is not suitable for objects of large dimensions because the steam shakes the clay creations, which damages them. After they have boiled, let them cool in the water.

Your hands are the main tools for working with polymer clay. The other simple pieces of equipment are: a knife, toothpicks, a glass jar to smooth the clay, and tinfoil—they are all most likely in your kitchen already!

Your hands and workspace must be washed thoroughly before beginning since this clay picks up every spot of dust and residue of other previously used colors.

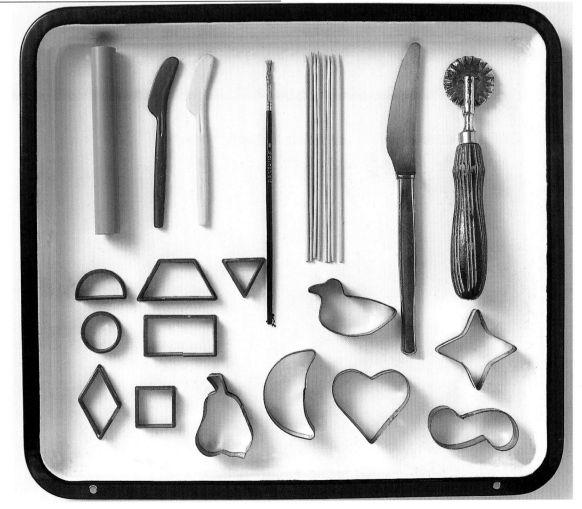

MARBLED NECKLACE

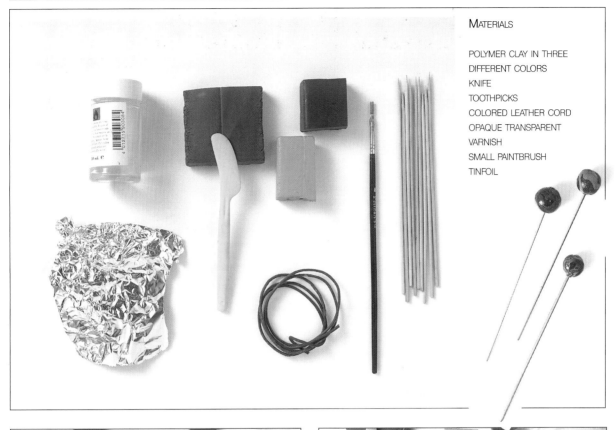

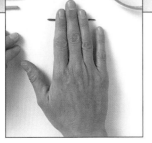

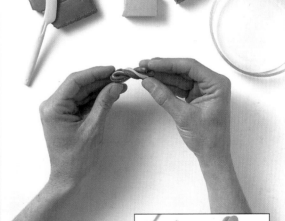

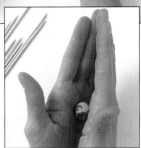

Take the three polymer clays (in this project: dark green, light blue, and purple). To create a marbled effect, make small cylinders of various sizes with each of the clays—big ones with the green, thin ones with the blue, and very thin ones with the purple. The more streaks you wish to have, the more different-sized colored cylinders you will have to prepare.

Wrap the cylinders around each other. Make a small ball and work it until you get the desired effect. The more you work the paste, the fewer streaks you will have since the colors tend to blend.

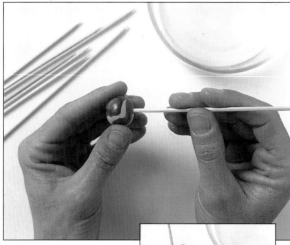

When the ball is finished, pierce it with a toothpick. Dampen your hands with cold water and smooth the surface with light pats so that you eliminate your finger marks.

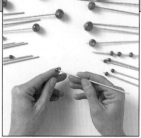

Repeat this operation and make all twenty marbled balls of decreasing sizes. Now, prepare nineteen (or twenty-one) with just one color (in this case purple). These should be all the same size and very small—they will separate the bigger beads from each other. Make three small green balls to use at the end as a clasp.

Take a baking tray, cover it with tinfoil, and place the prepared beads in it. Place the tray in the preheated oven. Bake the beads at a temperature between 212° F–248° F for five to ten minutes, according to their size. When baking beads for the first time, it is best to first experiment with some left over clay so that you get a better idea of when to turn off the heat. Too high of a temperature (it must never exceed 284° F) can cause flaking, cracking, or can alter the color. When the beads are ready, leave them to cool in the oven. Instead of being baked in the oven, beads can also be boiled in water for five minutes at a temperature of 212° F.

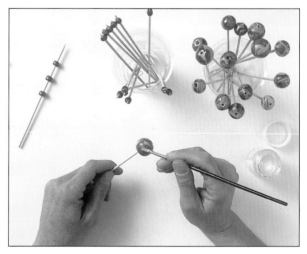

Once ready, this material can still be touched up. With a file or some sandpaper, you can refine the edges if they have any defects. Remember that abrasive rubbing will dull the colors.
To finish, a coat of transparent varnish will heighten the colors, which will have faded a little while being baked, and it also will protect the material. There are many brands of varnish on the market, so choose the one that is most suitable for the clays that you used.

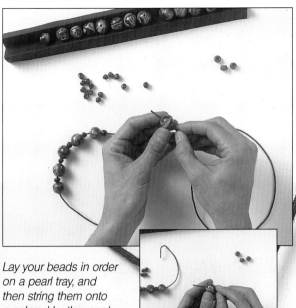

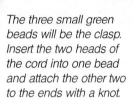

Lay your beads in order on a pearl tray, and then string them onto a colored leather cord, alternating each with a small purple bead.

The three small green beads will be the clasp. Insert the two heads of the cord into one bead and attach the other two to the ends with a knot.

Here are some other ideas for necklace clasps that were obtained with beads of the same material.

EARRINGS

Make a small ball and roll it out with a small rolling pin into a flat, circular shape.

Pierce it with a toothpick. Make another smaller ball and pierce it with a toothpick. Repeat these steps for the other earring. Bake in the oven and let cool. Coat the earrings with a glossy varnish to highlight the colors and to protect the clay.

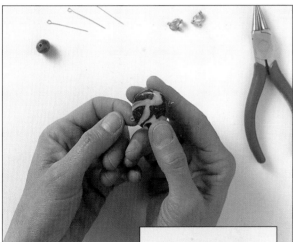

Insert an eye needle into the previously made hole and attach a ring to the end. Repeat this operation with the smaller bead. Hook the rings together.

Attach the earring clip.

JEWELRY DECORATED WITH ODDS AND ENDS

SAFETY PINS

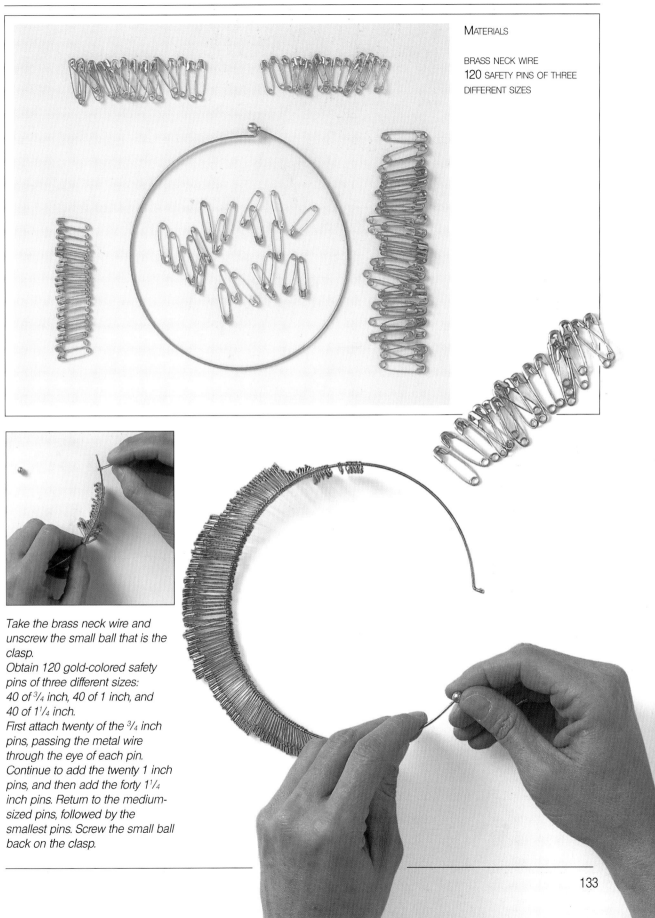

MATERIALS

BRASS NECK WIRE
120 SAFETY PINS OF THREE
DIFFERENT SIZES

Take the brass neck wire and unscrew the small ball that is the clasp.
Obtain 120 gold-colored safety pins of three different sizes: 40 of $3/4$ inch, 40 of 1 inch, and 40 of $1^1/4$ inch.
First attach twenty of the $3/4$ inch pins, passing the metal wire through the eye of each pin. Continue to add the twenty 1 inch pins, and then add the forty $1^1/4$ inch pins. Return to the medium-sized pins, followed by the smallest pins. Screw the small ball back on the clasp.

WOODEN TEES AND SHELLS

MATERIALS

12 WOODEN TEES (GOLF BALL PEGS)
WOODEN BEADS OF TWO SHAPES
NYLON THREAD
TWO SHELLS
BEAD REAMER
PINS
HAMMER
SCISSORS

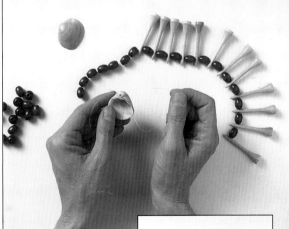

Obtain twelve wooden tees (golf ball pegs) and pierce a small hole in the thin ends. To do this, use a pin and lightly tap it with a hammer. Be careful because the wood could split if you tap too hard. String all the tees on the nylon thread, separating one from the other with an oval bead of amaranthine-colored glossy wood.

String another six beads on each side. Then string a shell with a small hole. Finish the necklace with nine round wooden beads. Knot the thread a couple of times and heat it with a flame to seal the nylon so that the knots will not open.

COLORED PENCILS

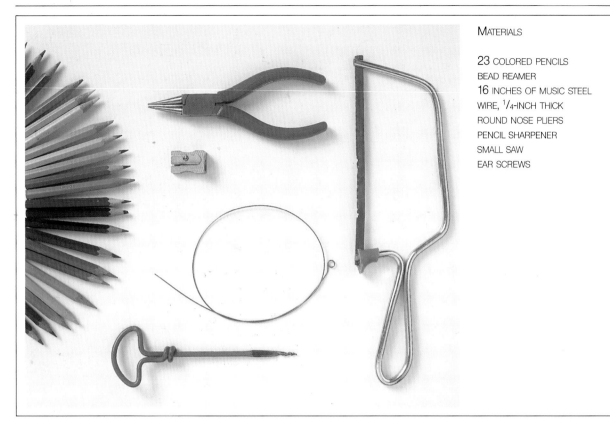

MATERIALS

23 COLORED PENCILS
BEAD REAMER
16 INCHES OF MUSIC STEEL
WIRE, 1/4-INCH THICK
ROUND NOSE PLIERS
PENCIL SHARPENER
SMALL SAW
EAR SCREWS

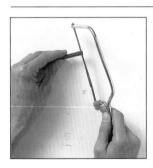

Take twenty-three old colored pencil stumps (if you do not have any, saw ordinary pencils at a length of 4 inches). Sharpen them until they measure 3 inches in length.

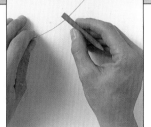

With the bead reamer, pierce a hole in each pencil at about ¹/₄ inch from the end. String the pencils along the wire, following the color scheme you prefer.

With the bead reamer, pierce a hole in each pencil at about ¹/₄ inch from the end. String the pencils along the wire, following the color scheme you prefer.

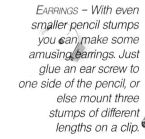

EARRINGS – With even smaller pencil stumps you can make some amusing earrings. Just glue an ear screw to one side of the pencil, or else mount three stumps of different lengths on a clip.

BARRETTE – You can make a very unusual barrette with thirteen well-sharpened pencil stumps. They can be in line, placed diagonally, or whatever way you like. When you have decided on the shape and color scheme, glue them onto an ordinary barrette.

ELECTRICAL MATERIALS

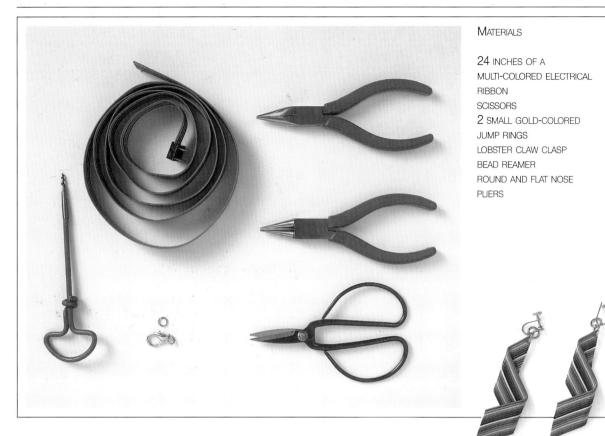

MATERIALS

24 INCHES OF A
MULTI-COLORED ELECTRICAL
RIBBON
SCISSORS
2 SMALL GOLD-COLORED
JUMP RINGS
LOBSTER CLAW CLASP
BEAD REAMER
ROUND AND FLAT NOSE
PLIERS

NECKLACE − *Cut the ends of the electrical ribbon diagonally and make a hole with the bead reamer on one end. Insert a jump ring.*

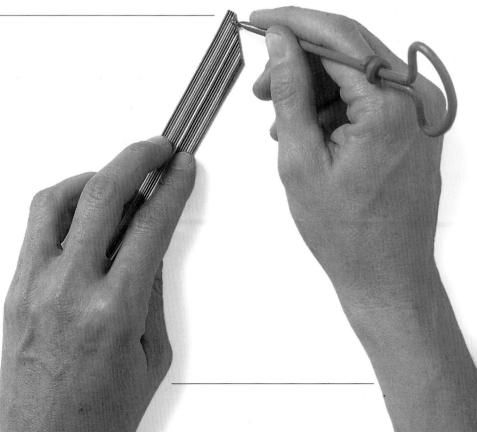

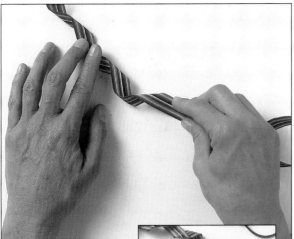

Make a row of hypen "V"- shaped folds all along the ribbon. Try to give this a round shape. The ribbon's copper core will hold the folds in shape.

Place a lobster claw clasp at the end.

EARRINGS – These are made by using the same technique as before. You will need two strips of ribbon that are 2^1/$_2$-inches long. Cut diagonally at the ends. Pierce one end and attach the earring clasp.

ANOTHER IDEA – Even small condensers can be used to make ornaments. If joined together they can make earrings; if attached to steel wire they can be charms. If placed side-by-side, they can be glued to a barrette.

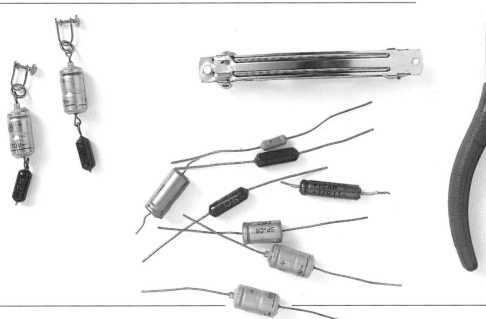

CRYSTAL

MATERIALS

8 CRYSTALS FROM A
CHANDELIER
16 INCHES OF MUSIC STEEL
NECK WIRE, 1/4-INCH THICK
FINE STEEL WIRE
ROUND NOSE PLIERS
GLASS BEADS
CRYSTAL PENDANT

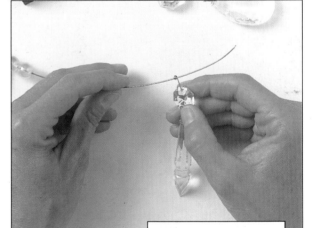

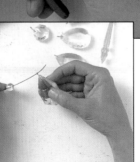

*NECKLACE – Lie the neck wire, the eight crystals, the glass beads, and the pendant on your workspace.
With the fine steel wire, make small hooks, which will be used to attach the crystals to the neck wire.*

String a small crystal, then a bead, then a bigger crystal, and so on until you reach halfway, where the pendant will be inserted. Repeat this sequence, stringing from the opposite side of the necklace.

EARRINGS – *Take two crystals, make a hook, and insert a small jump ring and ear screw.*

PASTA

Here is a fine array of original ornaments created with pasta pieces of various shapes and colors. Some twine or metal wire could be used to string them. It is fun to spice up the necklace with colored beads, seeds, or even metal studs.

MATERIALS

COLORED PASTA OF VARIOUS
SHAPES
COLORED COTTON CORD
ADHESIVE TAPE
SCISSORS

Cut a two-colored cotton cord to a length of 24 inches. Wrap one end with the adhesive tape.

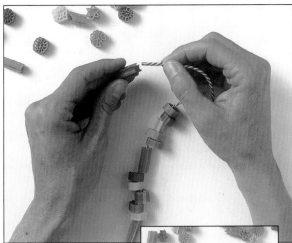

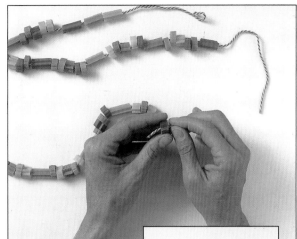

String the short pieces of pierced colored pasta, alternating the various shapes, for 16 inches.

Take another 20-inch cord and string on the pasta for about 12 inches.

Join the two rows with a knot on each side. Insert a piece of pasta on one side and make a loop on the other.

BUTTONS

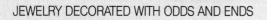

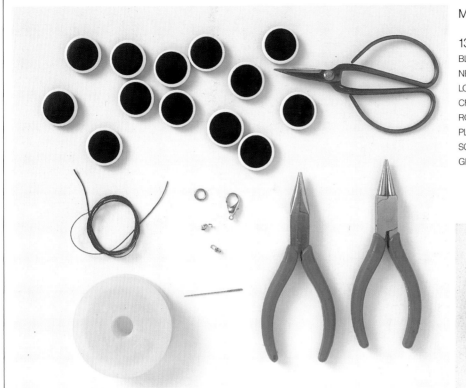

13 BUTTONS
BLACK WAX TWINE
NEEDLE
LOBSTER CLAW CLASP
CRIMP BEAD
ROUND AND FLAT NOSE
PLIERS
SCISSORS
GLUE

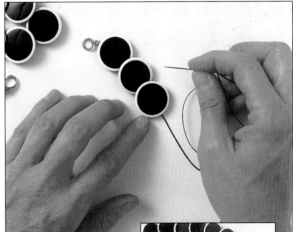

Attach a silver-colored crimp bead and lobster claw clasp to one end of the twine.

String thirteen buttons, making sure that each one slightly overlaps the next (make a knot after inserting each button). Attach another silver-colored crimp bead and a jump ring to finish and fasten the necklace.

Pins – Obtain a 5-inch pin, complete with safety cap. Take off the cap and insert a gold-colored metal bead. Attach it with a little bit of glue. Sew on a large button with a 1³/₄-inch diameter. Attach the seam with glue. Insert another two metal beads of different shapes and attach them with a drop of glue. Fasten the safety cap back on again.

BROOCHES, RINGS, AND BARRETTES

Two different techniques can be used to create these ornaments. The first consists of gluing the buttons onto the metal base. The second uses a strong thread, possibly colored, to sew the buttons on the clips or on rubber tubing. It is best to finish by gluing the ends of the thread to the base.

CANDY

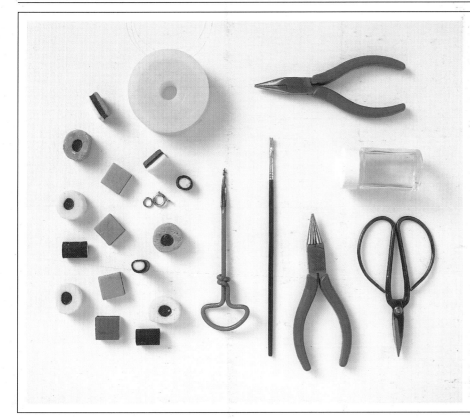

MATERIALS

40 COLORED CANDIES
NYLON THREAD
NEEDLE
BEAD REAMER
SPRING RING CLASP
OPAQUE TRANSPARENT
VARNISH
SMALL PAINTBRUSH
SCISSORS
ROUND AND FLAT NOSE
PLIERS

BARRETTE - With four candies shaped like squares, you can easily make an amusing barrette. Finish with transparent varnish.

Choose about forty licorice candies. Make a hole in each with the bead reamer and join the nylon thread to a clasp with knots.

String all the sweets, varying the colors and shapes. Attach a jump ring and fasten the spring ring clasp. With a small, flat paintbrush, spread a coat of transparent varnish to protect the sweets and particularly to prevent anyone from "tasting" one.

INDEX